50 Premium International Bread Baking Dishes

By: Kelly Johnson

Table of Contents

- French Brioche
- Italian Focaccia with Rosemary & Sea Salt
- Japanese Shokupan (Milk Bread)
- Indian Naan with Garlic Butter
- Turkish Simit (Sesame-Crusted Bread Rings)
- German Pretzels with Beer Cheese Dip
- Portuguese Broa (Corn Bread)
- Moroccan Msemen (Layered Flatbread)
- Mexican Bolillos (Crusty Rolls)
- Russian Borodinsky Bread (Rye & Coriander Loaf)
- Argentinian Fugazza (Cheese & Onion Flatbread)
- Ethiopian Injera (Teff Flour Fermented Flatbread)
- Swedish Kardemummabullar (Cardamom Buns)
- Greek Lagana (Olive Oil & Sesame Bread)
- Brazilian Pão de Queijo (Cheese Bread)
- Irish Soda Bread with Raisins & Caraway
- Danish Rugbrød (Dark Rye Bread)
- Persian Barbari Bread (Crispy Sesame Loaf)
- Chinese Scallion Pancakes
- Finnish Ruisleipä (Sourdough Rye Bread)
- Austrian Kaisersemmel (Emperor Rolls)
- Lebanese Manakish with Za'atar
- Cuban Pan Cubano (Crispy White Bread Loaf)
- Welsh Bara Brith (Tea-Soaked Fruit Bread)
- Korean Soboro Bread (Sweet Peanut Streusel Bun)
- Hungarian Kürtőskalács (Chimney Cake)
- Dutch Tiger Bread (Crispy Rice Coating)
- Scottish Bannock (Oatmeal Flatbread)
- South African Roosterkoek (Grilled Bread Rolls)
- Filipino Pandesal (Soft Bread Rolls)
- Ukrainian Paska (Easter Bread)
- Thai Roti (Flaky Flatbread)
- Romanian Cozonac (Sweet Walnut Swirl Bread)
- Icelandic Rúgbrauð (Steamed Dark Rye Bread)
- Norwegian Lefse (Potato Flatbread)

- Georgian Khachapuri (Cheese-Filled Bread)
- Serbian Pogacha (Traditional Round Bread)
- Polish Chleb Żytni (Rye Bread with Caraway)
- Pakistani Sheermal (Saffron-Scented Bread)
- Egyptian Aish Baladi (Whole Wheat Flatbread)
- Algerian Kesra (Semolina Flatbread)
- Hawaiian Sweet Bread Rolls
- Slovakian Vianočka (Braided Sweet Bread)
- Belarusian Perepecha (Filled Bread Rolls)
- Israeli Challah (Braided Egg Bread)
- Vietnamese Bánh Mì Baguette
- Syrian Tannour Bread (Clay Oven Flatbread)
- Czech Houska (Braided Bread with Poppy Seeds)
- Tibetan Tingmo (Steamed Bread Rolls)
- Malaysian Roti Jala (Lacy Bread Crepes)

French Brioche

Ingredients:

- 3 1/2 cups all-purpose flour
- 1/4 cup sugar
- 1 tsp salt
- 1 packet (2 1/4 tsp) yeast
- 4 eggs
- 1/2 cup warm milk
- 1 cup butter, softened
- 1 egg yolk + 1 tbsp milk (for egg wash)

Instructions:

1. Mix flour, sugar, salt, and yeast.
2. Add eggs and warm milk, then knead until combined.
3. Slowly incorporate butter, kneading for 10 minutes.
4. Cover and refrigerate overnight.
5. Shape into a loaf or rolls and let rise for 2 hours.
6. Brush with egg wash and bake at 375°F (190°C) for 25 minutes.

Italian Focaccia with Rosemary & Sea Salt

Ingredients:

- 3 1/2 cups all-purpose flour
- 1 packet (2 1/4 tsp) yeast
- 1 1/2 cups warm water
- 1/4 cup olive oil
- 1 tsp salt
- 2 tbsp fresh rosemary
- 1 tsp sea salt

Instructions:

1. Mix flour, yeast, warm water, and olive oil. Knead for 10 minutes.
2. Let dough rise for 1 hour.
3. Press dough into a baking sheet, dimple with fingers, and sprinkle rosemary and sea salt.
4. Bake at 400°F (200°C) for 20 minutes.

Japanese Shokupan (Milk Bread)

Ingredients:

- 3 1/2 cups bread flour
- 1/4 cup sugar
- 1 tsp salt
- 1 packet (2 1/4 tsp) yeast
- 1/2 cup warm milk
- 1/4 cup heavy cream
- 1 egg
- 2 tbsp butter

Instructions:

1. Mix flour, sugar, salt, and yeast.
2. Add milk, cream, and egg. Knead until smooth.
3. Knead in butter and let rise for 1 hour.
4. Shape into a loaf and let rise again.
5. Bake at 350°F (175°C) for 30 minutes.

Indian Naan with Garlic Butter

Ingredients:

- 3 cups all-purpose flour
- 1 packet (2 1/4 tsp) yeast
- 3/4 cup warm milk
- 1/4 cup yogurt
- 1 tsp salt
- 1 tbsp olive oil
- **For Garlic Butter:**
    - 2 tbsp butter, melted
    - 2 cloves garlic, minced

Instructions:

1. Mix flour, yeast, warm milk, yogurt, salt, and olive oil. Knead until smooth.
2. Let dough rise for 1 hour.
3. Divide into balls, roll out, and cook in a hot pan for 2 minutes per side.
4. Brush with garlic butter.

Turkish Simit (Sesame-Crusted Bread Rings)

Ingredients:

- 3 1/2 cups all-purpose flour
- 1 packet (2 1/4 tsp) yeast
- 1 cup warm water
- 2 tbsp olive oil
- 1 tsp salt
- 1/2 cup sesame seeds
- 1/4 cup molasses

Instructions:

1. Mix flour, yeast, water, olive oil, and salt. Knead until smooth.
2. Let rise for 1 hour.
3. Shape into rings, dip in molasses, and coat with sesame seeds.
4. Bake at 375°F (190°C) for 20 minutes.

German Pretzels with Beer Cheese Dip

Ingredients:

- 3 1/2 cups all-purpose flour
- 1 packet (2 1/4 tsp) yeast
- 1 cup warm water
- 1 tbsp sugar
- 1 tsp salt
- 1/4 cup baking soda (for boiling)
- **For Beer Cheese Dip:**
    - 1 cup shredded cheddar
    - 1/2 cup beer
    - 1 tsp mustard

Instructions:

1. Mix flour, yeast, water, sugar, and salt. Knead and let rise.
2. Shape into pretzels, boil in baking soda water, then bake at 400°F (200°C) for 15 minutes.
3. Simmer beer, cheddar, and mustard until smooth. Serve with pretzels.

Portuguese Broa (Corn Bread)

Ingredients:

- 2 cups cornmeal
- 1 cup all-purpose flour
- 1 packet (2 1/4 tsp) yeast
- 1 1/4 cups warm water
- 1 tsp salt

Instructions:

1. Mix flour, cornmeal, yeast, water, and salt. Knead into dough.
2. Let rise for 1 hour.
3. Shape into a round loaf and bake at 375°F (190°C) for 30 minutes.

Moroccan Msemen (Layered Flatbread)

Ingredients:

- 3 cups all-purpose flour
- 1/2 cup semolina
- 1/2 tsp salt
- 3/4 cup warm water
- 1/4 cup melted butter
- 1/4 cup olive oil

Instructions:

1. Mix flour, semolina, salt, and water. Knead and rest for 30 minutes.
2. Divide into balls, roll out thin, brush with butter and oil, fold, and flatten.
3. Cook on a hot pan for 2 minutes per side.

Mexican Bolillos (Crusty Rolls)

Ingredients:

- 3 1/2 cups all-purpose flour
- 1 packet (2 1/4 tsp) yeast
- 1 cup warm water
- 1 tsp salt
- 1 tbsp sugar

Instructions:

1. Mix flour, yeast, water, salt, and sugar. Knead and let rise.
2. Shape into small rolls and let rise again.
3. Bake at 400°F (200°C) for 20 minutes.

Russian Borodinsky Bread (Rye & Coriander Loaf)

Ingredients:

- 2 cups rye flour
- 1 cup whole wheat flour
- 1 packet (2 1/4 tsp) yeast
- 1/4 cup molasses
- 1 cup warm water
- 1 tbsp coriander seeds, crushed
- 1 tsp salt

Instructions:

1. Mix rye flour, whole wheat flour, yeast, molasses, warm water, and salt.
2. Knead into a sticky dough and let rise for 1 hour.
3. Shape into a loaf, sprinkle with coriander seeds, and let rise again.
4. Bake at 375°F (190°C) for 40 minutes.

Argentinian Fugazza (Cheese & Onion Flatbread)

Ingredients:

- 3 cups all-purpose flour
- 1 packet (2 1/4 tsp) yeast
- 1 cup warm water
- 1 tbsp olive oil
- 1/2 tsp salt
- 1 large onion, thinly sliced
- 1 cup mozzarella cheese, shredded
- 1 tsp oregano

Instructions:

1. Mix flour, yeast, warm water, olive oil, and salt. Knead and let rise.
2. Roll out dough into a pan and top with onions, cheese, and oregano.
3. Bake at 400°F (200°C) for 20 minutes.

Ethiopian Injera (Teff Flour Fermented Flatbread)

Ingredients:

- 2 cups teff flour
- 3 cups water
- 1/2 tsp salt
- 1/2 tsp baking soda

Instructions:

1. Mix teff flour and water, then let ferment at room temperature for 24–48 hours.
2. Stir in salt and baking soda before cooking.
3. Cook on a nonstick pan like a crepe, without flipping, until bubbles form.

Swedish Kardemummabullar (Cardamom Buns)

Ingredients:

- 3 1/2 cups all-purpose flour
- 1 packet (2 1/4 tsp) yeast
- 1/2 cup warm milk
- 1/4 cup sugar
- 1 tsp ground cardamom
- 1 egg
- 1/4 cup butter, melted

Instructions:

1. Mix flour, yeast, warm milk, sugar, cardamom, egg, and butter. Knead and let rise.
2. Roll out dough, spread with butter and sugar, fold, and cut into strips.
3. Twist and form into knots, then let rise again.
4. Bake at 375°F (190°C) for 15 minutes.

Greek Lagana (Olive Oil & Sesame Bread)

Ingredients:

- 3 1/2 cups all-purpose flour
- 1 packet (2 1/4 tsp) yeast
- 1 cup warm water
- 1/4 cup olive oil
- 1 tsp salt
- 2 tbsp sesame seeds

Instructions:

1. Mix flour, yeast, warm water, olive oil, and salt. Knead and let rise.
2. Roll out into a flat rectangle, sprinkle with sesame seeds, and dimple with fingers.
3. Bake at 375°F (190°C) for 25 minutes.

Brazilian Pão de Queijo (Cheese Bread)

Ingredients:

- 2 cups tapioca flour
- 1/2 cup milk
- 1/4 cup butter
- 1/2 tsp salt
- 1 cup shredded cheese (Parmesan or mozzarella)
- 1 egg

Instructions:

1. Heat milk, butter, and salt until warm.
2. Mix with tapioca flour, then add cheese and egg.
3. Shape into small balls and bake at 375°F (190°C) for 20 minutes.

Irish Soda Bread with Raisins & Caraway

Ingredients:

- 3 1/2 cups all-purpose flour
- 1 tsp baking soda
- 1/2 tsp salt
- 1 1/4 cups buttermilk
- 1/2 cup raisins
- 1 tsp caraway seeds

Instructions:

1. Mix flour, baking soda, and salt. Stir in buttermilk, raisins, and caraway seeds.
2. Shape into a round loaf and cut an "X" on top.
3. Bake at 375°F (190°C) for 40 minutes.

Danish Rugbrød (Dark Rye Bread)

Ingredients:

- 2 cups rye flour
- 1 cup whole wheat flour
- 1 packet (2 1/4 tsp) yeast
- 1 1/2 cups warm water
- 1/4 cup molasses
- 1/4 cup sunflower seeds
- 1 tsp salt

Instructions:

1. Mix flours, yeast, warm water, molasses, and salt. Knead into a dense dough.
2. Fold in sunflower seeds and let rise.
3. Shape into a loaf and bake at 350°F (175°C) for 50 minutes.

Persian Barbari Bread (Crispy Sesame Loaf)

Ingredients:

- 3 1/2 cups all-purpose flour
- 1 packet (2 1/4 tsp) yeast
- 1 cup warm water
- 1/2 tsp salt
- 1 tbsp sesame seeds

Instructions:

1. Mix flour, yeast, warm water, and salt. Knead and let rise.
2. Roll into long ovals, brush with water, and sprinkle sesame seeds.
3. Bake at 400°F (200°C) for 20 minutes.

Chinese Scallion Pancakes

Ingredients:

- 2 cups all-purpose flour
- 3/4 cup hot water
- 1/2 tsp salt
- 1/2 cup chopped scallions
- 1 tbsp sesame oil

Instructions:

1. Mix flour, hot water, and salt into a dough. Rest for 30 minutes.
2. Roll out, brush with sesame oil, sprinkle scallions, roll up, and flatten.
3. Cook on a hot pan for 2 minutes per side.

Finnish Ruisleipä (Sourdough Rye Bread)

Ingredients:

- 2 cups rye flour
- 1 cup all-purpose flour
- 1/2 cup sourdough starter
- 1 1/2 cups warm water
- 1 tsp salt

Instructions:

1. Mix flours, starter, water, and salt into a sticky dough. Let rest for 1 hour.
2. Knead lightly, then cover and ferment at room temperature for 12–24 hours.
3. Shape into a round loaf and proof for another 2 hours.
4. Bake at 375°F (190°C) for 40 minutes.

Austrian Kaisersemmel (Emperor Rolls)

Ingredients:

- 3 1/2 cups all-purpose flour
- 1 packet (2 1/4 tsp) yeast
- 1 cup warm water
- 1 tbsp butter, melted
- 1 tsp salt
- 1 tsp sugar

Instructions:

1. Mix flour, yeast, warm water, butter, salt, and sugar. Knead and let rise for 1 hour.
2. Shape into rolls and press a Kaiser stamp or fold by hand. Let rise again.
3. Bake at 400°F (200°C) for 15 minutes.

Lebanese Manakish with Za'atar

Ingredients:

- 3 cups all-purpose flour
- 1 packet (2 1/4 tsp) yeast
- 1 cup warm water
- 1/4 cup olive oil
- 1 tsp salt
- **For Topping:**
    - 2 tbsp za'atar
    - 2 tbsp olive oil

Instructions:

1. Mix flour, yeast, water, olive oil, and salt. Knead and let rise.
2. Roll into circles and spread with za'atar mixed with olive oil.
3. Bake at 375°F (190°C) for 15 minutes.

Cuban Pan Cubano (Crispy White Bread Loaf)

Ingredients:

- 3 1/2 cups bread flour
- 1 packet (2 1/4 tsp) yeast
- 1 cup warm water
- 1 tbsp sugar
- 1 tbsp lard or butter
- 1 tsp salt

Instructions:

1. Mix flour, yeast, water, sugar, lard, and salt. Knead and let rise for 1 hour.
2. Shape into loaves and let rise again.
3. Bake at 375°F (190°C) for 25 minutes.

Welsh Bara Brith (Tea-Soaked Fruit Bread)

Ingredients:

- 2 cups dried fruit (raisins, currants)
- 1 cup hot black tea
- 3 cups self-rising flour
- 1/2 cup brown sugar
- 1 egg
- 1 tsp cinnamon

Instructions:

1. Soak dried fruit in tea overnight.
2. Mix soaked fruit, flour, sugar, egg, and cinnamon.
3. Pour into a loaf pan and bake at 350°F (175°C) for 50 minutes.

Korean Soboro Bread (Sweet Peanut Streusel Bun)

Ingredients:

- **For Dough:**
    - 3 cups bread flour
    - 1 packet (2 1/4 tsp) yeast
    - 3/4 cup warm milk
    - 1/4 cup sugar
    - 1 egg
    - 2 tbsp butter
- **For Streusel:**
    - 1/4 cup flour
    - 1/4 cup sugar
    - 2 tbsp butter
    - 2 tbsp crushed peanuts

Instructions:

1. Mix dough ingredients and knead. Let rise for 1 hour.
2. Mix streusel ingredients until crumbly.
3. Shape dough into buns, top with streusel, and bake at 375°F (190°C) for 15 minutes.

Hungarian Kürtőskalács (Chimney Cake)

Ingredients:

- 3 1/2 cups all-purpose flour
- 1 packet (2 1/4 tsp) yeast
- 3/4 cup warm milk
- 1/4 cup sugar
- 2 tbsp butter
- 1 egg
- **For Coating:**
    - 1/2 cup sugar
    - 1 tsp cinnamon
    - 2 tbsp melted butter

Instructions:

1. Mix dough ingredients, knead, and let rise for 1 hour.
2. Roll into strips, wrap around a greased rolling pin, and brush with melted butter.
3. Coat with cinnamon sugar and bake at 375°F (190°C) for 15 minutes.

Dutch Tiger Bread (Crispy Rice Coating)

Ingredients:

- **For Dough:**
    - 3 1/2 cups all-purpose flour
    - 1 packet (2 1/4 tsp) yeast
    - 1 cup warm water
    - 1 tbsp sugar
    - 1 tsp salt
- **For Coating:**
    - 1/2 cup rice flour
    - 1/2 cup warm water
    - 1 tbsp sugar
    - 1/2 tsp salt

Instructions:

1. Mix dough ingredients, knead, and let rise for 1 hour.
2. Mix coating ingredients and spread over shaped dough.
3. Bake at 375°F (190°C) for 25 minutes.

Scottish Bannock (Oatmeal Flatbread)

Ingredients:

- 2 cups oat flour
- 1/2 cup all-purpose flour
- 1 tsp baking soda
- 1/2 tsp salt
- 3/4 cup buttermilk

Instructions:

1. Mix dry ingredients, then stir in buttermilk to form a dough.
2. Flatten into a round and cook in a dry skillet for 5 minutes per side.

South African Roosterkoek (Grilled Bread Rolls)

Ingredients:

- 3 cups bread flour
- 1 packet (2 1/4 tsp) yeast
- 1 cup warm water
- 1 tbsp sugar
- 1 tsp salt

Instructions:

1. Mix flour, yeast, warm water, sugar, and salt. Knead and let rise for 1 hour.
2. Shape into rolls and grill over medium heat for 5 minutes per side.

Filipino Pandesal (Soft Bread Rolls)

Ingredients:

- 3 1/2 cups all-purpose flour
- 1 packet (2 1/4 tsp) yeast
- 1 cup warm milk
- 1/4 cup sugar
- 1 tsp salt
- 1 egg
- 1/4 cup butter, melted
- 1/2 cup breadcrumbs (for coating)

Instructions:

1. Mix flour, yeast, warm milk, sugar, salt, egg, and butter. Knead until smooth.
2. Let rise for 1 hour.
3. Shape into small rolls, coat with breadcrumbs, and let rise again.
4. Bake at 350°F (175°C) for 20 minutes.

Ukrainian Paska (Easter Bread)

Ingredients:

- 4 cups all-purpose flour
- 1 packet (2 1/4 tsp) yeast
- 1 cup warm milk
- 1/2 cup sugar
- 1/4 cup butter, melted
- 2 eggs
- 1 tsp vanilla extract

Instructions:

1. Mix flour, yeast, warm milk, sugar, butter, eggs, and vanilla. Knead and let rise.
2. Shape into a round loaf with braided decorations on top. Let rise again.
3. Bake at 375°F (190°C) for 30 minutes.

Thai Roti (Flaky Flatbread)

Ingredients:

- 2 cups all-purpose flour
- 1/2 cup water
- 1 tbsp condensed milk
- 2 tbsp butter, melted
- 1/4 tsp salt

Instructions:

1. Mix flour, water, condensed milk, butter, and salt into a soft dough. Rest for 30 minutes.
2. Divide into balls, roll out thin, and cook in a hot pan for 2 minutes per side.

Romanian Cozonac (Sweet Walnut Swirl Bread)

Ingredients:

- 4 cups all-purpose flour
- 1 packet (2 1/4 tsp) yeast
- 3/4 cup warm milk
- 1/2 cup sugar
- 1/4 cup butter, melted
- 2 eggs
- **For Filling:**
    - 1 cup ground walnuts
    - 1/4 cup sugar
    - 1 tsp cocoa powder

Instructions:

1. Mix dough ingredients, knead, and let rise.
2. Roll out dough, spread with walnut filling, and roll up.
3. Let rise again and bake at 375°F (190°C) for 35 minutes.

Icelandic Rúgbrauð (Steamed Dark Rye Bread)

Ingredients:

- 2 cups rye flour
- 1 cup whole wheat flour
- 1 tsp baking soda
- 1/2 tsp salt
- 1/2 cup molasses
- 1 1/2 cups buttermilk

Instructions:

1. Mix all ingredients into a thick batter.
2. Pour into a greased loaf pan, cover tightly, and steam over low heat for 8 hours.

Norwegian Lefse (Potato Flatbread)

Ingredients:

- 2 cups mashed potatoes
- 1 cup all-purpose flour
- 1/2 tsp salt
- 1 tbsp butter, melted

Instructions:

1. Mix mashed potatoes, flour, salt, and butter.
2. Roll into thin rounds and cook on a dry skillet for 1–2 minutes per side.

Georgian Khachapuri (Cheese-Filled Bread)

Ingredients:

- 3 cups all-purpose flour
- 1 packet (2 1/4 tsp) yeast
- 3/4 cup warm milk
- 1/4 cup butter, melted
- 1 cup shredded cheese (feta, mozzarella)
- 1 egg (for topping)

Instructions:

1. Mix dough ingredients and let rise.
2. Shape into a boat, fill with cheese, and bake at 375°F (190°C) for 15 minutes.
3. Crack an egg on top and bake for another 5 minutes.

Serbian Pogacha (Traditional Round Bread)

Ingredients:

- 3 1/2 cups all-purpose flour
- 1 packet (2 1/4 tsp) yeast
- 1 cup warm milk
- 1 tbsp sugar
- 1/2 tsp salt
- 1/4 cup butter, melted

Instructions:

1. Mix flour, yeast, warm milk, sugar, salt, and butter. Knead and let rise.
2. Shape into a round loaf and let rise again.
3. Bake at 375°F (190°C) for 30 minutes.

Polish Chleb Żytni (Rye Bread with Caraway)

Ingredients:

- 2 cups rye flour
- 1 cup bread flour
- 1 packet (2 1/4 tsp) yeast
- 1 cup warm water
- 1 tbsp caraway seeds
- 1 tsp salt

Instructions:

1. Mix flours, yeast, warm water, caraway seeds, and salt. Knead and let rise.
2. Shape into a loaf and let rise again.
3. Bake at 375°F (190°C) for 40 minutes.

Pakistani Sheermal (Saffron-Scented Bread)

Ingredients:

- 3 cups all-purpose flour
- 1 packet (2 1/4 tsp) yeast
- 3/4 cup warm milk
- 1/4 cup sugar
- 1/4 cup butter, melted
- 1/4 tsp saffron

Instructions:

1. Mix flour, yeast, warm milk, sugar, butter, and saffron. Knead and let rise.
2. Shape into a round flatbread and let rise again.
3. Bake at 375°F (190°C) for 20 minutes.

Egyptian Aish Baladi (Whole Wheat Flatbread)

Ingredients:

- 2 cups whole wheat flour
- 1 cup all-purpose flour
- 1 packet (2 1/4 tsp) yeast
- 1 cup warm water
- 1/2 tsp salt

Instructions:

1. Mix flours, yeast, warm water, and salt. Knead and let rise.
2. Divide into balls, roll out, and bake at 450°F (230°C) for 5 minutes.

Algerian Kesra (Semolina Flatbread)

Ingredients:

- 2 cups fine semolina
- 1/2 cup all-purpose flour
- 1/2 tsp salt
- 1/2 cup warm water
- 2 tbsp olive oil

Instructions:

1. Mix semolina, flour, salt, water, and olive oil into a dough.
2. Roll into a thin round and prick with a fork.
3. Cook on a hot griddle for 3–4 minutes per side.

Hawaiian Sweet Bread Rolls

Ingredients:

- 3 1/2 cups all-purpose flour
- 1 packet (2 1/4 tsp) yeast
- 3/4 cup warm pineapple juice
- 1/4 cup sugar
- 1/4 cup butter, melted
- 1 egg
- 1/2 tsp salt

Instructions:

1. Mix flour, yeast, pineapple juice, sugar, butter, egg, and salt. Knead and let rise.
2. Shape into rolls and let rise again.
3. Bake at 350°F (175°C) for 20 minutes.

Slovakian Vianočka (Braided Sweet Bread)

Ingredients:

- 4 cups all-purpose flour
- 1 packet (2 1/4 tsp) yeast
- 1 cup warm milk
- 1/2 cup sugar
- 1/4 cup butter, melted
- 2 eggs
- 1 tsp vanilla extract

Instructions:

1. Mix flour, yeast, milk, sugar, butter, eggs, and vanilla. Knead and let rise.
2. Divide into three strands, braid, and let rise again.
3. Bake at 375°F (190°C) for 30 minutes.

Belarusian Perepecha (Filled Bread Rolls)

Ingredients:

- 3 1/2 cups all-purpose flour
- 1 packet (2 1/4 tsp) yeast
- 1 cup warm milk
- 1/4 cup sugar
- 1/4 cup butter, melted
- **For Filling:**
    - 1 cup mashed potatoes or sweet cheese

Instructions:

1. Mix dough ingredients, knead, and let rise.
2. Divide, fill with mashed potatoes or cheese, and seal into rolls.
3. Let rise again and bake at 375°F (190°C) for 20 minutes.

Israeli Challah (Braided Egg Bread)

Ingredients:

- 4 cups all-purpose flour
- 1 packet (2 1/4 tsp) yeast
- 1 cup warm water
- 1/4 cup honey
- 1/4 cup vegetable oil
- 2 eggs
- 1 tsp salt

Instructions:

1. Mix flour, yeast, warm water, honey, oil, eggs, and salt. Knead and let rise.
2. Braid into a loaf and let rise again.
3. Bake at 375°F (190°C) for 30 minutes.

Vietnamese Bánh Mì Baguette

Ingredients:

- 3 1/2 cups bread flour
- 1 packet (2 1/4 tsp) yeast
- 1 cup warm water
- 1 tsp sugar
- 1/2 tsp salt

Instructions:

1. Mix flour, yeast, warm water, sugar, and salt. Knead and let rise.
2. Shape into baguettes and let rise again.
3. Bake at 450°F (230°C) for 20 minutes.

Syrian Tannour Bread (Clay Oven Flatbread)

Ingredients:

- 3 cups all-purpose flour
- 1 packet (2 1/4 tsp) yeast
- 1 cup warm water
- 1/2 tsp salt

Instructions:

1. Mix flour, yeast, warm water, and salt. Knead and let rise.
2. Roll into thin rounds and bake in a very hot oven (or clay oven) for 3 minutes.

Czech Houska (Braided Bread with Poppy Seeds)

Ingredients:

- 3 1/2 cups all-purpose flour
- 1 packet (2 1/4 tsp) yeast
- 1 cup warm milk
- 1/4 cup sugar
- 1/4 cup butter, melted
- 1 egg
- 1 tbsp poppy seeds

Instructions:

1. Mix flour, yeast, warm milk, sugar, butter, and egg. Knead and let rise.
2. Shape into a braided loaf and sprinkle with poppy seeds. Let rise again.
3. Bake at 375°F (190°C) for 30 minutes.

Tibetan Tingmo (Steamed Bread Rolls)

Ingredients:

- 3 cups all-purpose flour
- 1 packet (2 1/4 tsp) yeast
- 3/4 cup warm water
- 1/2 tsp salt
- 1 tbsp oil

Instructions:

1. Mix flour, yeast, warm water, salt, and oil. Knead and let rise.
2. Shape into rolls and let rise again.
3. Steam for 20 minutes.

Malaysian Roti Jala (Lacy Bread Crepes)

Ingredients:

- 1 cup all-purpose flour
- 1 cup coconut milk
- 1 egg
- 1/4 tsp salt
- 1/4 cup water

Instructions:

1. Mix all ingredients into a smooth batter.
2. Pour through a perforated bottle or squeeze bottle onto a hot pan in a lace pattern.
3. Cook for 1 minute, fold, and serve.

www.ingramcontent.com/pod-product-compliance
Lightning Source LLC
LaVergne TN
LVHW081500060526
838201LV00056BA/2851